# My WEIGHTLIFTING Coloring Book

Author - **Ivan R. Rojas** • Illustrator - **Michael Diniz Swingler**

Copyright 2018 by Ivan Rojas
The book author retains sole copyright to
his contributions to this book.

Published 2018.
Printed in the United States of America.

All rights reserved.

No portion of this book may be reproduced, stored in a retrieval system, or transmitted in any form or by any means – electronic, mechanical, photocopy, recording, scanning, or other – except for brief quotations in critical reviews or articles, without the prior written permission of the author.

ISBN 978-1-943650-91-0

This book was published by BookCrafters,
Parker, Colorado
www.bookcrafters.net

# My Weightlifting coloring book...

## Dedication

*To my little buddy Rey Alberto Rodriguez Rios...*

Pablo Picasso once said, "Every child is an artist. The problem is how to remind an artist once he grows-up." One afternoon, while coaching in Panama, I met Rey Alberto (eight years old then). Out of the blue, he told me, "I want to shoot down UFO's with a bazooka," and he was serious about it! That imagination, that innocence, that expression of complete possibility, inspired me to write this book. I thought that I should do something for girls and boys around the world. I want kids to know how big the world is, and how they can achieve their dreams. This coloring book is an opportunity for every child to learn about world geography and weightlifting, while enjoying art. This book is suitable to also help children learn English.

*The Clean & Jerk*

# Equipment

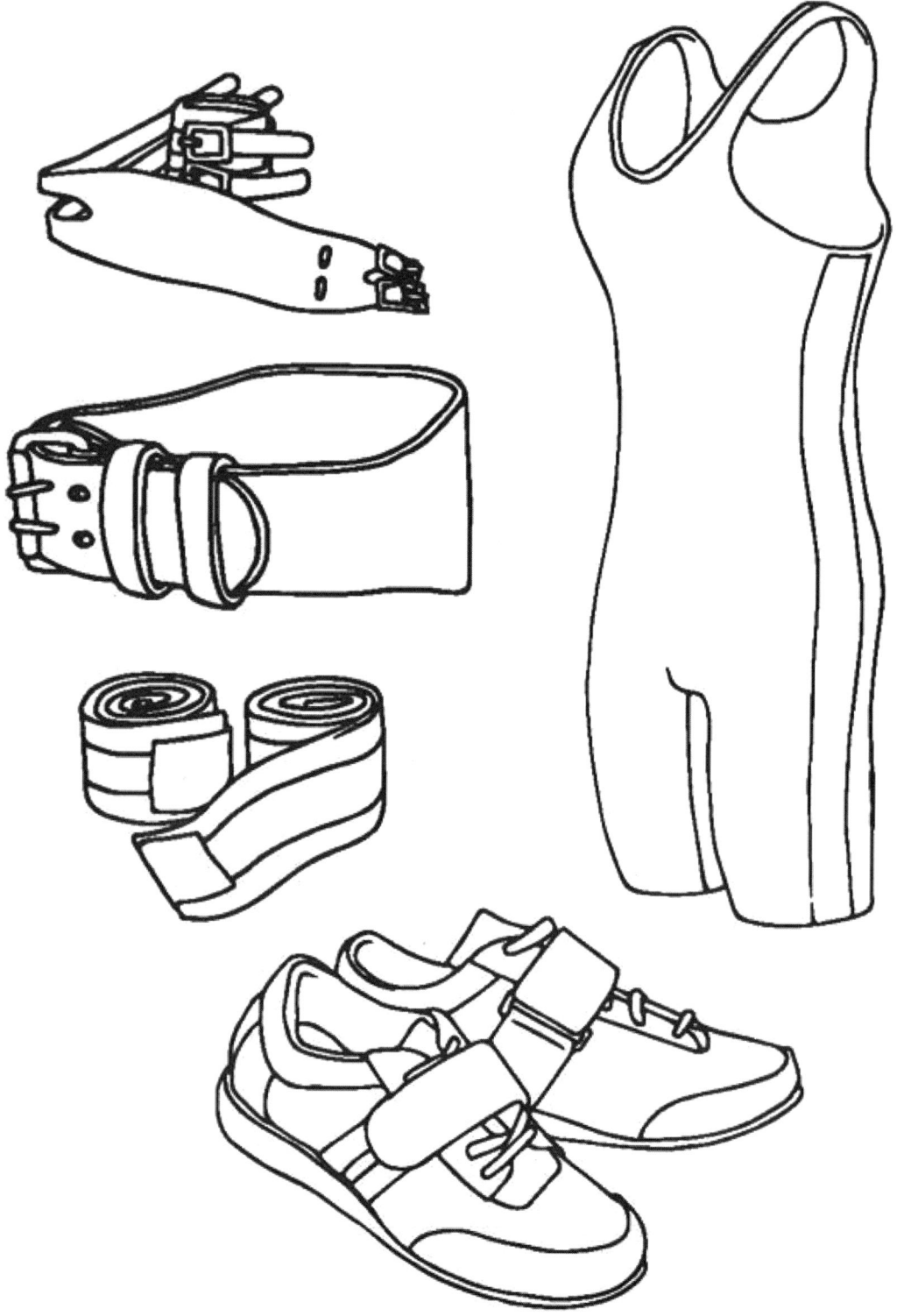

# Bar, bumpers and platform

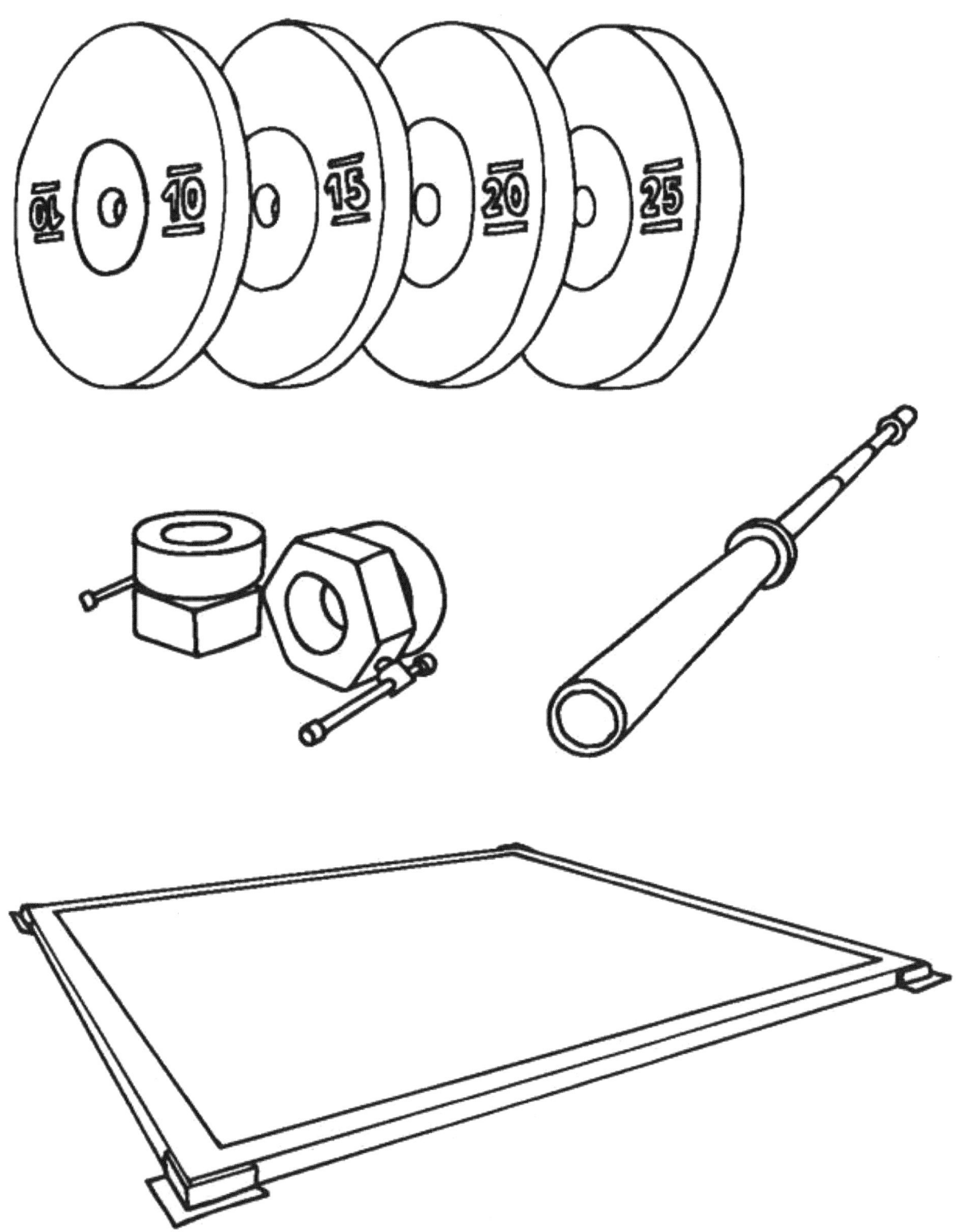

*Elio Guerra*

| | |
|---|---|
| Best snatch | 159 kgs |
| Best C & J | 191 kgs |
| Cat. | 85 kgs |
| CUBA | |

## CUBA

Cuba is an island located in Central America

| | |
|---|---|
| Capital | Havana |
| Official language | Spanish |
| Demonym | Cuban |
| Population | |
| 2017 Census | 11,221,060 |
| Currency | Peso |
| Calling code | +53 |

*Oscar Figueroa*

Best snatch 142 kg
Best C & J 177 Kg
Cat 62 Kg
Colombia

## COLOMBIA

Colombia is a country located in South America

| | |
|---|---|
| Capital | Bogota |
| Official language | Spanish |
| Demonym | Colombian |
| Population | |
| 2018 estimate | 49,913,668 |
| Currency | Peso |
| Calling code | +57 |

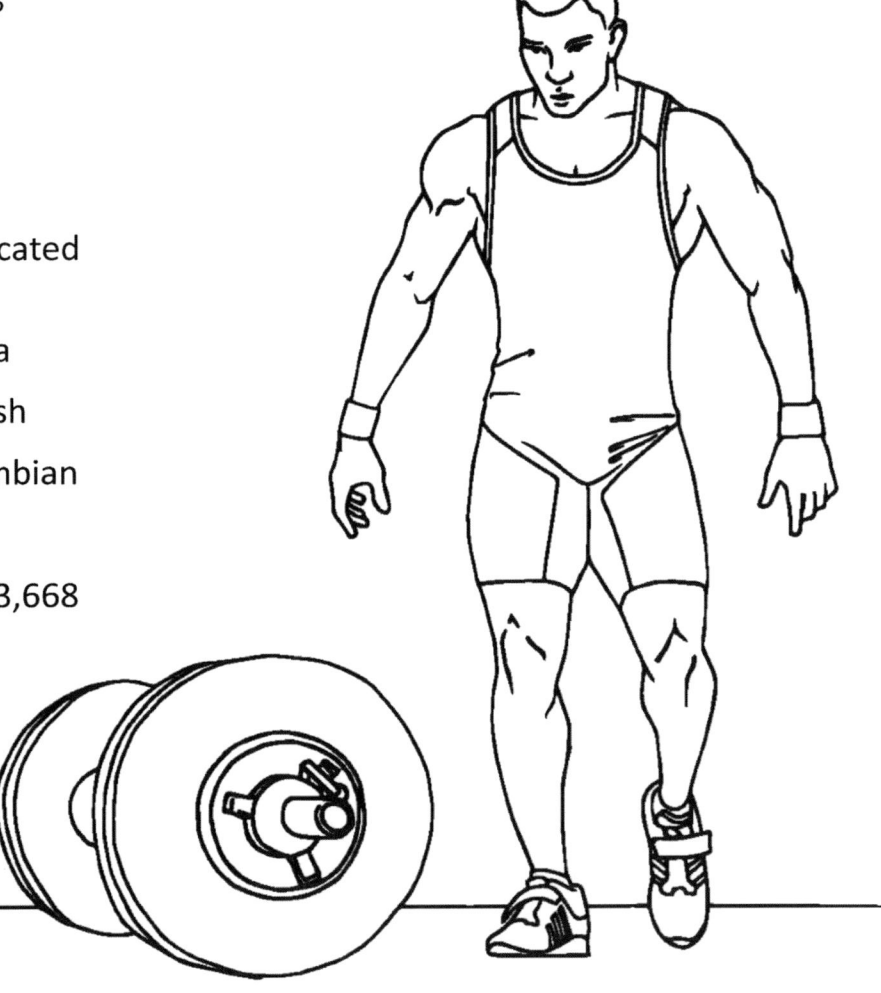

*Lidia Valentin*
Best Snatch 122 Kg
Best C&J    147 Kg
Cat 75 Kg
Spain

## *Spain*

Spain is a country in Europe.

| | |
|---|---|
| Capital | Madrid |
| Language | Spanish |
| Demonym | Spanish – Spaniard |
| Population 2018 estimate | 46,700,000 |
| Currency | Euro |
| Calling Code | +34 |

*Arley Mendez Perez*
Best Snatch   175 Kg
Best C&J      212 Kg
Cat 85 Kg
Chile

# *Chile*

**Chile is a country in south America**

Capital       Santiago

Language   Spanish

Demonym   Chilean

Population

2017 Census 17,574,003

Currency     Chilean Peso

Calling code  +56

*Shi Zhiyong*
Best snatch 162 Kg
Best C & J    190 Kg
Cat 69 Kg
China

# China

China is a country in East Asia.

| | |
|---|---|
| Capital | Beijing |
| Language | Chinese |
| Demonym | Chinese |
| Currency | Renminbi (RMB) |
| Population | |
| Population | |
| 2018 estimate | 1,403,500,365 |
| Calling code | +86 |

*Won Jeong-sik*
Best Snatch  148 kgs
Best C & J    178 kgs
Cat 69 Kg
South Korea

## South Korea

Officially the Republic of Korea, is a country in East Asia.

Capital      Seoul

Language   Korean

Demonym   South Korean
             Korean

Population

2017 estimate 51,446,201

Currency    South Korean
             Won

Calling code   +82

*Neisi Dajomes*
Best Snatch 115 kg
Best C & J   140 kg
Cat 75 kg
Ecuador

## ECUADOR

**Officially the Republic of Ecuador, is a country in northwestern South America.**

*Capital     Quito*

*Language  Spanish*

*Demonym  Ecuadorian*

*Population*

*2016 estimate 16,385,068*

*Currency    US Dollar*

*Calling Code + 593*

*Mohamed Ihab*
Best Snatch 165 kg
Best C & J    201 kg
Cat  77 Kg
Egypt

# Egypt

The Arab Republic of Egypt is a country in the northeast corner of Africa.

| | |
|---|---|
| Capital | Cairo |
| Language | Arabic |
| Demonym | Egyptian |
| Population | |
| 2017 census | 94,798,827 |
| Currency | Egyptian pound |
| Calling code | +20 |

## CJ Cummings
Best snatch  143 kg
Best C & J     185 kg
Cat 69 kg
USA

# *USA*

USA is a country in North America

Capital         Washington DC

Language     English

Demonym     American

Currency       US Dollar

Population

2017 estimate 325,719,538

Calling Code  +1

*Gwendolyn Sisto*
Best snatch    92 Kg
Best C & J    110Kg
Cat 69 kg
USA

# USA

USA is a country in North America

Capital    Washington DC

Language    English

Demonym    American

Currency    US Dollar

Population

2017 estimate 325,719,538

Calling Code  +1

*Ivan Efremov*
Best Snatch 182 Kg
Best C & J 218 Kg
Cat 105 Kg
Uzbekistan

## *Uzbekistan*

Uzbekistan is a country in Asia.

Capital     Tashkent

Language    Uzbek, Russian

Demonym     Uzbek

Currency    Som

Population

2017 estimate 32,979,000

Calling code  +998

*Lasha Talakhadse*
Best Snatch  220 Kg
Best C & J    258 Kg
Cat +105 Kg
Georgia

# *Georgia*

Georgia is a country in the Caucasus region of Eurasia.

| | |
|---|---|
| Capital | Tbilisi |
| Language | Georgian |
| Demonym | Georgian |
| Currency | Georgian Lari |

Population

2017 estimate 3,718,200

Calling code   +995

*Aurimas Didzbalis*
Best Snatch 176 kg
Best C & J 212
cat 94Kg
Lithuania

## *Lithuania*

Lithuania is a country in Europe.

Capital    Vilnius

Language   Lithuanian

Demonym    Lithuanian

Currency   Euro

           Lithuanian litas

Population

2017 estimate 2,800,667

Calling code    +370

*Kianoush Rostami*
Best Snatch 179 kg
Best C&J 220 Kg
Cat 85 kg
Iran

# *Iran*

Iran is a country in Asia.

| | |
|---|---|
| Capital | Tehran |
| Language | Persian |
| Demonym | Iranian |
| Currency | Rial |

Population

2018 estimate   81,672,300

Calling code   +98

*Fernado Reis*
Best Snatch 200 Kg
Best C&J     240 kg
cat +105 kg
Brazil

# Brazil

Brazil is a country in South America.

| | |
|---|---|
| Capital | Brasilia |
| Language | Portuguese |
| Demonym | Brazilian |
| Currency | Real |
| Population | |
| 2019 estimate | 210,147,125 |
| Calling code | +55 |

*Loredana-Elena Toma*
Best snatch 109 kg
Best C & J 128 Kg
cat 63 Kg
Romania

# *Romania*

Romania is a country in Europe

| | |
|---|---|
| Capital | Bucharest |
| Language | Romanian |
| Demonym | Romanian |
| Currency | Leu |

Population

2017 estimate  19,638,000

Calling code  +40

*Chanu Saikhom Mirabai*
Best Snatch 86 Kg
Best C & J 110 Kg
India

## *India*

India is a country in Asia.

Capital        New Delhi

Language    Hindi – English

Demonym    Indian

Currency      Rupee

Population

2016 estimate
1,324,171,354

Calling code  +91

*Sopita Tanasan*
Best Snatch 96 Kg
Best C & J 114 Kg
Cat 53 Kg
Thailand

# *Thailand*

Thailand is a country in Asia.

| | |
|---|---|
| Capital | Bangkok |
| Language | Thai |
| Demonym | Thai |
| Currency | Baht |
| Population | |
| 2016 estimate | 68,863,514 |
| Calling code | +66 |

*Kim Tuan Thach*
Best snatch 135 Kg
Best C & J  161 Kg
Cat 56 Kg
Vietnam

# *Vietnam*

Vietnam is a country in Asia.

Capital     Hanoi

Language    Vietnamese

Demonym     Vietnamese

Currency    Dong

Population

2016 estimate 94,569,072

Calling Code +84

The author may be contacted by email at:
ivan.rojas01@yahoo.com

*My Weightlifting Coloring Book* is available from
all online bookstores.
Bulk orders may be placed by contacting the author.

Other titles by this author:

9781943650071 - *Kazakhstan Weightlifting System for Elite Athletes*
Gwendolyn Sisto & Ivan Rojas
9781943650408 - *Fundamentals of the Soviet System*: The Soviet Weightlifting System
Gwendolyn Sisto & Ivan Rojas

CPSIA information can be obtained
at www.ICGtesting.com
Printed in the USA
LVRC022333291018
595212LV00013B/184